EXTREME SURVIVAL

ANIMAL SURVIVAL

Lori Hile

Raintree

Chicago, Illinois

www.heinemannraintree.com
Visit our website to find out
more information about
Heinemann-Raintree books.

To order:

☎ Phone 888-454-2279
💻 Visit www.heinemannraintree.com
to browse our catalog and order online.

© 2011 Raintree
an imprint of Capstone Global Library, LLC
Chicago, Illinois

Visit our website at
www.heinemannraintree.com

Edited by Adam Miller, Adrian Vigliano, and Andrew
Farrow
Designed by Steve Mead
Original illustrations © Capstone Global Library Ltd.
Illustrated by Jeff Edwards
Picture research by Tracy Cummins
Production by Camilla Crask
Originated by Capstone Global Library Ltd
Printed and bound in the United States of America,
North Mankato, MN

15 14 13 12 11
10 9 8 7 6 5 4 3 2 1

Library of Congress Cataloging-in-Publication Data
Hile, Lori.
  Animal survival / Lori Hile.
    p. cm.—(Extreme survival)
  Includes bibliographical references and index.
  ISBN 978-1-4109-3973-9 (hc)
  ISBN 978-1-4109-3980-7 (pb)
 1. Pets—Anecdotes—Juvenile literature. 2.
Animals—Anecdotes—Juvenile literature. 3. Animal
heroes—Anecdotes—Juvenile literature. 4. Natural
disasters—Environmental aspects—Juvenile
literature. 5. Animal behavior—Juvenile literature. I.
Title.

  SF416.2.H56 2011
  591.5—dc22   2010028842

Acknowledgments
The author and publishers are grateful to the
following for permission to reproduce copyright
material: Alamy p. **46** (©BRIAN ELLIOTT); AP Photo
pp. **45** (Daytona Beach News-Journal/ Nigel Cook),
28 (The Detroit News/Mark Hicks), **22** (Karel
Prinsloo), **36** (Kyodo News), **49** (Richard Lam), **44**
(Todd Plitt); Corbis pp. **17**, **30** (©Arnd Wiegmann/
Reuters), **47** (©Barnabas Honeczy/epa/), **26** (©HO/
Reuters), **23** (©Hulton-Deutsch Collection), **18**
(©LEE CELANO/Reuters), **25** (©Staffan Widstrand),
12 (©Toni Albir/epa), **37** (©ZSOLT SZIGETVARY/
epa); Flickr p. **33** (Thomas Schrantz); Getty Images
pp. **19** (Atomare Aufruestung), **41** (Christian Science
Monitor), **16** (Comstock Images), **4** (Matt Cardy),
48 (Spencer Platt); istockphoto p. **27** (©Wesley
Tolhurst); Landov p. **20** (SUE COCKING/MCT/Miami
Herald); ©Mirrorpix p. **29**; National Geographic
Stock p. **15** (Katherine Feng/Minden Pictures);
Naturepl.com pp. **38** & **39** (Lynn M. Stone); Rex
Features pp. **9** (Daryl Wright/Newspix), **10** (Derek
Cattani), **11** (Derek Cattani); Shutterstock pp. **7**
(©Sirko Hartmann), **40** (©Four Oaks), **42** & **43**
(©Chris Hill); ZUMA Press p. **34** (The San Diego
Union Tribune).

Cover photograph of a dogsled team reproduced
with the permission of Photolibrary/Hskan Hjort.

We would like to thank Ann Fullick for her invaluable
help in the preparation of this book.

Every effort has been made to contact copyright
holders of any material reproduced in this book. Any
omissions will be rectified in subsequent printings if
notice is given to the publisher.

Disclaimer
All the Internet addresses (URLs) given in this book
were valid at the time of going to press. However,
due to the dynamic nature of the Internet, some
addresses may have changed, or sites may have
changed or ceased to exist since publication. While
the author and publisher regret any inconvenience
this may cause readers, no responsibility for any
such changes can be accepted by either the author
or the publisher.

CONTENTS

ANIMALS BEATING THE ODDS 4

INTO THE WILD: WILDERNESS SURVIVAL 6

SURVIVING NATURAL DISASTERS 14

THE HUMAN THREAT 22

ACCIDENTS AND ABANDONMENT 28

INCREDIBLE JOURNEYS 32

WITH A LITTLE HELP FROM THEIR FRIENDS 38

ANIMAL HEROES 42

MORE ANIMAL SURVIVAL FACTS 50

GLOSSARY 52

FIND OUT MORE 54

INDEX 56

Some words are printed in bold, **like this**. You can find out what they mean by looking in the glossary.

ANIMALS BEATING THE ODDS

Earthquakes. Wars. Burning buildings. Deserted islands. Freezing temperatures. The cats, dogs, dolphins, elephants, and other creatures in this book have all encountered these extreme situations!

They have faced natural disasters like **hurricanes** and **tsunamis**. They have experienced accidents, like falling overboard, getting lost, and even being flushed down the toilet. And they have endured dangers created by humans, such as wars, hunting, and the destruction of their **habitats**.

A worker with England's National Seal Sanctuary helps rescue an injured seal in 2009.

Beating the odds

But the animals in these true stories all have one thing in common. They all beat the odds to survive. Some have even rescued humans or other animals from danger.

You will meet Scarlett, the mother cat that pulled her kittens from a burning building. You will learn how Molly the pony survived a devastating hurricane and the loss of a leg. You will follow Bobbie "the wonder dog" as he crisscrossed an entire country, trying to track down his owners. You will meet a sturdy pelican that survived a war. And these are just a few of the world's many animal survivors.

How do they do it?

The animals discussed here are remarkable. But they often use abilities that most animals— even your own pets—already possess. They rely on their super-sharp senses. They act out of **instinct**, meaning they react without thinking. And they employ some special skills that even scientists cannot fully explain. But one thing is for certain. When faced with challenges, these animals have taken survival to extremes. These are their dramatic, real-life stories.

LEARN MORE ABOUT . . .

>> Do husky dogs have a secret weapon against the cold? Read about Taro and Jiro on page 8.

>> Can animals predict earthquakes? Learn from China's baby pandas on page 14.

>> Can a polar bear cub survive without its mother? Read more on page 30.

>> How do animals return home from miles away? Follow one on page 32.

>> Can dogs detect cancer? Flip to page 46 and read about George.

INTO THE WILD: WILDERNESS SURVIVAL

Imagine that your pet dog is stranded on a desert island. Could she survive? Or could she live through the coldest winter on Earth? Wild animals learn how to fight other animals that attack, and they also learn how to hunt for food. But most pets never need to learn these skills.

The following are true-life tales of animals that were raised by humans, but then forced to live in the wild.

Extreme temperatures

In February 1958, a group of Japanese scientists was working at a research base on the continent of Antarctica. Suddenly, a fierce blizzard blew in. The snowstorm forced the scientists to **evacuate** the base by helicopter. But there was no room on the helicopter for their 15 husky sled dogs. A relief team was scheduled to arrive at the base in a few days. So, the scientists left the dogs tightly chained up outside, with a small supply of food and water. Unfortunately, the bad weather continued for months, and the new team never made it to the base.

The researchers did not expect the dogs to live through the Antarctic winter—where temperatures can dip as low as −90 °C (−130 °F). The dogs had never survived on their own in the wild. A year later, Kitagawa, one of the dog handlers, returned. He thought he would bury his beloved dogs. But when he arrived, he was shocked to find two of the dogs, Taro and Jiro, waiting there to greet him. Remarkably, they had unchained themselves and kept themselves alive. The scientists believed that the two dogs banded together to kill and eat penguins, seals, and perhaps sea lions for food during the long, cold winter.

HUSKIES

Huskies are among the world's best athletes. They are able to run long distances twice as fast as humans. This ability probably helped Taro and Jiro hunt slower animals, like penguins and seals. Huskies also have two incredibly thick layers of fur. These act like a permanent fur coat with a fuzzy sweater underneath. Still, it is rare for huskies to survive such harsh conditions for more than a month.

Survivor: Australia

If Sophie Tucker were human, she would probably be a star contestant on the television reality show Survivor. But Sophie is an Australian cattle dog. In November 2008, Sophie went sailing with her owners, Jan and Dave Griffith, off the east coast of Queensland, Australia. Rough waters rocked the boat, and Sophie fell overboard. The Griffiths spent over an hour searching for their dog, but found no trace of her. They returned home, in tears, forced to assume that Sophie had drowned.

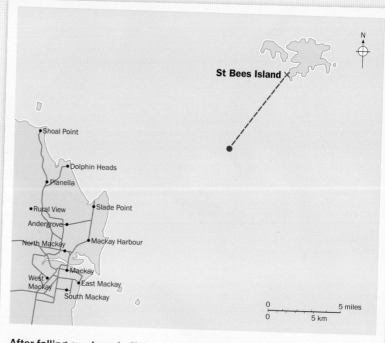

After falling overboard off the coast of Australia, Sophie swam nearly six miles to St Bees Island.

Four months later, the Griffiths heard that park rangers had found a dog on a small island. They did not believe it could really be Sophie. But they contacted the rangers and agreed to meet the dog. When the Griffiths approached, the dog started whimpering and pawing at her cage. Sure enough, it was Sophie! When Sophie's cage was opened, she excitedly jumped on the Griffiths.

SURVIVAL SCIENCE

Relying on instinct

Even though Sophie never had to kill for food before, her dog and wolf **ancestors** (relatives from long ago) did. Faced with starvation, Sophie called upon her basic survival **instincts**. Baby goats are small and weak, so it was probably easy for Sophie to hunt them down.

The will to survive

It turns out that Sophie was tougher and smarter than the Griffiths had realized. She had dog-paddled her way just over 9 kilometers (almost 6 miles), through shark-filled waters, until she reached land. She had landed on St Bees Island, a place filled with wild goats, koalas, and a few people. When locals first spotted Sophie, she was thin and mangy. But after a few weeks, Sophie began looking plump and healthy. Residents found the remains of baby goats. They realized that Sophie had begun killing the goats for food.

Sophie was in remarkably good condition when she returned. "She didn't even smell," said Jan. Apparently Sophie took regular swims off the island beach. But Sophie was happy to leave her wild ways behind. She now enjoys lounging in the Griffiths' air-conditioned house and devouring doggie treats.

"She surprised us all. She was a house dog, and look what she's done: she has swum over five nautical miles. She has managed to live off the land all on her own."

—Jan Griffith, Sophie Tucker's owner

Here is Sophie, safely back with Jan Griffith after returning from St Bees Island.

A lion named Christian

Some animals have been raised by humans, but they truly belong in the wild. This was the case for a lion named Christian.

In 1969 two young Australian men, Anthony (Ace for short) and John, were living in London, England. They saw Christian, a lion cub, in a cage at Harrods department store—and he was for sale! The friends began coming every day to play with the lion. One day they had the crazy idea to buy him.

When Christian was a cub, Ace and John were able to keep him happy in their small apartment and in the furniture store below, where both of them worked. Christian became famous and attracted lots of people to the store to see him. But as the lion grew bigger, Ace and John knew they would need to find Christian a new home. In those days, zoo cages were small, so the men did not think Christian would be happy there.

Fortunately, two actors walked into the furniture store at the right moment. They had starred in the movie *Born Free*, the true story of a lioness that was introduced into the wild by a couple named George and Joy Adamson. The actors put Ace and John in touch with George Adamson, who agreed to train Christian to survive in the wild. The young men brought Christian to Kenya, in Africa. There, he learned how to hunt and communicate with other lions. Then, he was released into the wild.

NO SALE

Today, laws protect lions from being sold at places like department stores.

Christian as a cub with Ace and John in the furniture store where the men worked.

From department store cub to king of the jungle

Ace and John returned to Kenya a year later to look for Christian. After Ace and John called Christian's name, the lion hesitated only a moment before bounding over to them. He jumped into their arms and knocked them down with hugs. The men visited Christian again a few years later. By then, Christian was the leader of his **pride** (group of lions) and the largest lion around. But he still remembered the friends who set him free.

SURVIVAL SCIENCE

Lion in training

When Christian arrived in Kenya, he had a lot to learn about living in the wild. He had to **adapt** to (get used to) the hot African afternoons. He had to toughen his paws, which were more familiar with plush carpet than rough jungle. He had to learn how to band together with other lions, rather than humans, in a pride. Most importantly, Christian had to learn to stalk and kill other animals for food.

Christian warmly welcomes a visit from his friends after a year in the wilds of Kenya.

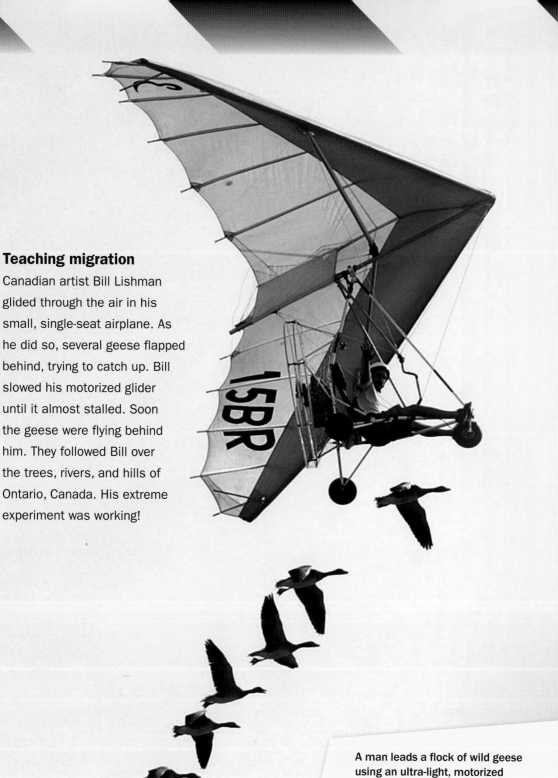

Teaching migration

Canadian artist Bill Lishman glided through the air in his small, single-seat airplane. As he did so, several geese flapped behind, trying to catch up. Bill slowed his motorized glider until it almost stalled. Soon the geese were flying behind him. They followed Bill over the trees, rivers, and hills of Ontario, Canada. His extreme experiment was working!

A man leads a flock of wild geese using an ultra-light, motorized glider. Since some birds follow gliders, Bill Lishman wondered if he could use this to teach them.

Bill's goal was to teach birds to **migrate**. He wanted them to move to a warmer, southern area when it got too cold in Canada. Most birds learn to migrate from their parents. But those that are orphaned or raised in **captivity** (enclosed areas) do not learn how. When released into the wild, many of these birds cannot survive the cold, northern winters. If Bill could teach birds to migrate, many birds would be saved.

So, Bill bought Canada goose eggs. When the eggs hatched, he taught the goslings that he was their "father." Newborn birds will follow the first moving object they see. The geese followed him everywhere, even when he soared through the air in his plane.

In 1993, after years of trial and error, Bill led 18 Canada geese from his home in northern Ontario all the way to Virginia—650 kilometers (400 miles) south. The next spring, the birds returned to Bill's property on their own!

RARE BIRDS

In 1941 there were only 21 whooping cranes in existence. Now, 377 whooping cranes live in the wild, with the number gradually increasing. Whooping cranes are still **endangered**. But the **species** stands a better chance of survival thanks to Bill Lishman's experiments.

SURVIVAL SCIENCE

How do birds find their way home?

During the day, birds may use the sun's position as a compass. At night, they are likely guided by the placement of the stars. On cloudy days (and nights), birds sometimes use the wind to help navigate. They also may rely on their strong sense of smell.

And some birds—along with a few other species, including whales, dolphins, and bats—have something in their brains, called **magnetite**, that is attracted to magnets. Scientists believe that this mineral helps birds align themselves with Earth's **magnetic field**. Magnetic fields include the areas where the attraction or repulsion of magnets are felt. Earth is like a special magnet. Forces called magnetic field lines surround the planet. These forces cause compass needles to point north. The magnetite in birds' brains responds to the pull of the magnetic field, providing the creatures with a built-in compass.

SURVIVING NATURAL DISASTERS

Most animals spend a lot of time in nature. But does this prepare animals to deal with natural disasters? The animals in these stories were put to the test.

Out of an earthquake

On May 12, 2008, the giant panda cubs in China's Wolong National Nature Reserve were acting strangely. Some paced back and forth on the grass. Others climbed up trees and refused to come down.

A few hours later, the mountains that towered over the reserve started to rumble. Trees, dirt, and boulders the size of cars came tumbling down. It was the biggest earthquake to hit China in 30 years, and the **epicenter** (origin) of the quake was located in western China, right near the reserve.

SURVIVAL SCIENCE

Can animals predict natural disasters?

Many animals, including fish, earthworms, dogs, cats, and bears, act oddly before some natural disasters. Can these animals somehow sense the coming danger? Some scientists believe that animals can feel the **electromagnetic waves** that are released before a thunderstorm or earthquake. These are invisible waves of energy. Certain fish have receptors on their backs to detect these waves, while other animals use sensors on their eyes, tongues, whiskers, or fur. In China, scientists have **evacuated** people from four different villages when they observed animals behaving strangely. There was only one false alarm.

The park rangers tried to lead the baby pandas to safety. But they were trapped. Boulders blocked the path to the village's main road. So, the panda keepers created a different—and dangerous—new route. It involved balancing along a high, narrow wall and climbing a ladder to a rain-soaked bridge. The handlers tucked the scared little pandas under their arms and carried them up the path to safety.

Although thousands of people were hurt or killed in the earthquake, all 13 panda babies survived. There are only 1,600 pandas left in the wild, and all of them live in western China. This made it especially important to protect the pandas at Wolong Reserve. A big loss would have threatened the survival of the entire **species**.

These giant panda cubs are playing near a huge landslide in Wolong Reserve, shortly after the 2008 earthquake.

Owen and Mzee

On December 26, 2004, an enormous earthquake rumbled under the Indian Ocean. This set off giant sets of waves called **tsunamis**. The enormous size and force of the waves flooded countries along the Indian Ocean, killing about 230,000 people.

By December 27, 2004, tsunami waves had come and gone in Kenya. But a baby hippo was left stranded on a coral reef in the Indian Ocean.

He could not reach the shore on his own. So, dozens of townspeople used ropes, nets, fishing boats, and even cars to try to rescue the hippo. It was not easy, since hippos can be aggressive when they feel threatened. But a boy named Owen managed to tackle the baby hippo, while someone else draped a strong shark net over the animal's body. The hippo, soon nicknamed "Owen" after the brave boy, was lifted into a truck and carted off to a nearby animal park.

SURVIVAL SCIENCE

Owen's chances of survival

Why was Owen put in a park, instead of released back into the wild? Without his family, Owen would have had to either survive on his own or join a new group of hippos. Since Owen was still a baby, he had not yet learned how to fend for himself. And hippos not familiar with Owen would have seen him as an intruder and attacked him. The park was Owen's best hope for survival.

Hippos spend time together in the wild, in groups called pods. But adult male (bull) hippos are very territorial, and younger males may be attacked if a bull thinks he is being challenged.

Hippo meets tortoise

There were concerns that Owen would not be safe with strange adult hippos. So, he was placed in a large enclosure with a giant Aldabra tortoise named Mzee. Mzee was over 100 years old and liked to keep to himself. But as soon as Owen saw the tortoise, he ran over and crouched down beside him. Mzee hissed at Owen and crept away—but Owen was faster than the old tortoise and continued to follow him around. By the end of the evening, Owen slept cuddled next to Mzee.

The park rangers were still worried. Owen was not eating the leaves they left out for him. Without a mother to learn from, it was possible that Owen simply did not know what to do. But when Mzee sat down next to Owen and started munching the leaves, Owen began to eat, too. After losing his family in the tsunami, Owen's unlikely friendship with Mzee helped save his life. The two remain friends.

SURVIVAL SCIENCE

Finding a parent

Why did Owen bond so quickly with Mzee? Scientists believe it is because the tortoise's grayish coloring and rounded shape resemble that of a hippo. Alone and scared, Owen needed a parent. He probably latched onto the first thing that looked like one.

Owen the hippo cuddles up to Mzee, his 130-year-old tortoise friend.

Surviving Katrina

Hurricane Katrina was one of the worst natural disasters ever to strike the United States. In August 2005, the violent storm swept through the Gulf Coast of the United States, from central Florida to Texas. The hurricane devastated large areas along the coast with strong winds and floods, hitting the city of New Orleans, Louisiana, especially hard.

When residents left to escape the rising water, many were forced to abandon their pets. Most people could not return home for weeks. This left thousands of pets trapped in homes filling up with water.

STATS

KATRINA BY THE NUMBERS

The following are statistics about animals affected by Hurricane Katrina:

Number of pets stranded in New Orleans: 50,000–100,000

Number of pets that were rescued: 10,000–15,000

Number of pets reunited with their owners: 2,000–3,000

Number of pets adopted or awaiting adoption: 8,000–12,000

Number of animal rescue groups involved: Over 20

Number of animal rescue volunteers involved: Over 5,000

A dog escapes flood waters in New Orleans, eight days after Katrina struck.

Bob and Bobbi: Best friends forever

In the wake of Hurricane Katrina, a dog and a cat were left behind in New Orleans. The dog was tied to a post outside a house. The cat stayed by her side. They waited for someone to feed them, but no one came. After a few days, the dog broke free from the post, and the pair set off to find food. No one knows exactly what happened next, but the pets probably faced packs of hungry dogs, deserted streets, and dirty water.

They must have found scraps of food because, somehow, they managed to survive on their own . . . for four months! That is when a construction worker spotted the pair and noticed how thin they were. He cut off the dog's chain, fed the pets, and brought them to a shelter. At the shelter, the pets were given their new names: Bob Cat and Bobbi Dog, because both of them had "bobbed" tails. Volunteers at the shelter soon realized that Bob Cat was blind. All this time, Bobbi the dog had been the cat's seeing-eye dog! Without him, the cat almost certainly would have died.

After their story was covered on television, many people wanted to adopt the two Bobbies. An owner was carefully selected. The pair lived together and even shared the same bowl of milk, until Bob the cat died in late 2008.

SURVIVAL SCIENCE

Unnatural friends?

Cats and dogs are not necessarily enemies, but they're not always friends either. Many starving dogs hunted cats to eat after Hurricane Katrina. But because Bob and Bobbi lived together before the hurricane, they probably felt a strong bond. This contributed to their devoted friendship and their survival.

Molly the pony

Molly, an Appaloosa pony, has two survival tales. She was found in a barn two weeks after Hurricane Katrina. She had survived by drinking dirty water and eating hay. After Molly was adopted and moved to a new farm, a dog bit her leg so deeply that Molly could barely stand. Many horses with broken legs are put to sleep, because healing takes a very long time—and the chances of infection and re-injury are great. But Molly's owner decided to try an experimental new treatment.

Molly's hurt leg was **amputated** (cut off) from the knee down, and a **prosthesis** (fake limb) was attached to the stump where her leg ended. It took a while for Molly to adjust to the new "leg," which looks a bit like a toilet plunger. But now Molly trots around the farm and visits with kids who wear prosthetic limbs, just like she does. Molly's fake leg leaves a footprint that looks like a smiley face.

Molly's prosthetic leg doesn't keep the pony from greeting visitors.

George and Frisky: Saving each other

A man named George adopted a puppy named Frisky after the puppy showed up on his doorstep in Biloxi, Mississippi. That was 19 years before Katrina. By 2005 George was almost 80 years old, and Frisky was 19 and nearly blind. When Katrina struck, George's house started to fill with water.

As the level rose, Frisky floated on an old mattress, but George was too heavy. To keep his head above the liquid, George had to tread water. As the night wore on, George almost gave up—but every time he stopped moving, Frisky leaned over and licked his owner's face to wake him up and keep him going. After 12 hours, the water level lowered, both George and Frisky made it to the hospital to recover.

UNCONDITIONAL LOVE

After Katrina, there were more pets left in New Orleans than there were people able to care for them. So, the city got creative. A group of rescued pets was transferred to Dixon Correctional Facility, a prison about two hours from New Orleans. There, the prisoners had nothing but time to take care of the critters, and the pets badly needed care. But the prisoners perhaps needed the pets just as much. Richard Palmer, who served 13 years at the prison, said, "The dogs teach us things . . . about love and patience. The dogs appreciate us, and we appreciate them." He loved one dog in particular, named Papi, and vowed to adopt the terrier after he had served his time. Today, Richard and his wife are Papi's proud owners.

THE HUMAN THREAT

*Animals survive in the wild by constantly **adapting** their behavior to the conditions around them. But what if their surroundings are threatened? This can happen when forests are cut down, hunters kill animals, or wars spread into wilderness areas. Can animals adapt when humans invade their **habitats**?*

The war-zone pelican

In March 2003, the U.S. Army invaded the Middle Eastern country of Iraq. The city of Baghdad was left in tatters. The Baghdad Zoo was spared, but most of the zookeepers had fled for their safety. In April a U.S. Army captain named William Sumner was sent to the zoo to try to restore order. What he found was heartbreaking. Many of the cages were found empty, and many animals that were still there were in bad condition. One of the saddest sites was a pelican tied to a pole with a 1-meter (3-foot) piece of rope. The pelican could not move around. The water bird had only dirty rainwater to drink, and no water to swim or bathe in. But he survived.

The captain and a team of animal volunteers built a pelican pond out of sandbags, a tarp (large piece of material), and a couple of hoses. The pelican dove into the pond immediately and stayed for days. Gradually, his health came back. And soon other pelicans were brought in to join him. The zoo re-opened three months later.

A worker at the Baghdad Zoo helps clean the newly built pelican pond. After building the pond, volunteers brought in more pelicans to join the one that survived the abandonment of the zoo.

Beauty and the Blitz

In late 1940, Nazi Germany bombed London for 57 straight nights. This series of attacks, known as "the Blitz," reduced buildings to rubble. Many people were hurt or killed, and many pets were trapped under the destroyed buildings. A group called the People's Dispensary for Sick Animals sent rescue squads to look for hurt pets.

Beauty, a wire-haired terrier, often accompanied worker Bill Barnett on his searches. One night, Beauty started digging in the debris alongside Bill. Within a few minutes, she uncovered a cat buried beneath a table. During her wartime career, Beauty rescued a total of 63 animals. Her work made people realize that animals could aid in "search and rescue" missions.

Beauty the terrier helps owner Bill Barnett sniff for animals trapped under rubble in London.

Miza the Gorilla

In 2007 a ranger at Virunga Park, Congo, in Africa, climbed up and down the mountain, making calming gorilla noises. But he could not find Miza or her mother, Lessinjina. The two mountain gorillas had been missing for several days. Miza's father, Kabirizi, was hidden in the trees, tending to the rest of his large family. But soon Kabirizi strode off in search of the pair. After a few days, the ranger saw Kabirizi back with his pack. Crouching behind him was a small set of eyes—Miza! But Miza's mother was not with her. Since mother gorillas almost never leave their babies alone, it was likely that Lessinjina was killed by hunters, or by soldiers fighting nearby.

Without her mother, Miza refused to eat. Her hair started falling out, and the skin on her hands turned red and rough. The park ranger had to decide. Should he let Miza learn to eat on her own, or should he feed her himself? If he left Miza alone, she could die. But if Miza never learned to eat on her own, she would have to spend her life in a hospital for orphaned gorillas. The ranger decided to leave the baby alone. Fortunately, Miza's older sister helped feed her baby sister bamboo until Miza grew stronger. Soon, the little gorilla was swinging from vines and leaping from branches. Even though humans destroyed her mother, Miza would survive.

SURVIVAL SCIENCE

Maternal bonds

Baby gorillas are fed their mother's milk for the first two and a half years of life. They also stay with their mothers for three to four years. Miza was just under two years old when she was orphaned, which is why the loss of her mother was especially difficult. But adult male gorillas also make good parents. They are protective and often help raise babies.

HOW TO SAVE THE MOUNTAIN GORILLA

There are only 700 mountain gorillas left on the planet. You could fit all of them into the space of about 10 classrooms. They are threatened mainly by human diseases and human activities like war, hunting, and cutting down trees. Parks are working to protect the gorillas from illegal hunting by hiring more park rangers. They are also limiting how long tourists are allowed to visit with the animals, to stop the spread of human diseases like strep throat and measles, which can kill gorillas.

A baby mountain gorilla munches a piece of bark. There are only 700 mountain gorillas left in the wild, which means rangers are especially concerned about the survival of each one.

Escaping bushfire: Cinders, the koala that could

Smoke filled the forest in Australia. Giant flames covered the **bush** (forested wilderness). Fire rolled up tree trunks and devoured eucalyptus leaves. Cowering at the top of a tall tree was a mother koala named Cinders, and her joey (baby koala). Koalas run slowly, so all Cinders could do was climb higher. Fortunately, her tree was in a "fire break," an area cleared of bush. The fire lost fuel before it reached Cinders. But Cinders's ordeal was far from over.

Cinders and her joey were hungry, but most of their feeding trees had burned down in the fire. Too big to fit in Cinders's pouch, the joey clung to Cinders's back as her mother slid down the tree. For hours, Cinders padded past burned bushes, fields, dry riverbeds, and across highways, sniffing for the sweet smell of eucalyptus. She traveled 19 kilometers (12 miles) until she spotted what she wanted: a swamp mahogany tree (a kind of eucalyptus).

But a dog started barking. Cinders was in someone's backyard! A girl called her dog in, but stared at the koala in surprise. Koalas are common in Australia, but mostly in the bush and zoos—not in neighborhoods. Cinders climbed up the tree and feasted on eucalyptus leaves while her joey nursed. After a few days, neighbors watched as Cinders waddled on her way to a forest, where she and her joey would have their choice of over 50 varieties of eucalyptus leaves.

A firefighter nurses a koala back to health after a bush fire.

SURVIVAL SCIENCE

The eucalyptus diet
A koala's diet consists almost entirely of leaves from eucalyptus trees—about 1,000 leaves, or 1 kilogram (2 pounds), per day. That is why these trees are so important to koalas. Eucalyptus leaves contain almost 50 percent water, so koalas rarely have to drink.

DISAPPEARING FORESTS

Brush fires are a major threat to eucalyptus trees. They are caused by lightning strikes, campfires, or other fires, and then they are spread by the wind. But humans are also a threat. People cut down the trees for wood and use oil from the leaves for cough drops and insect repellents. As cities spread out, more trees are chopped down.

With fewer trees, koalas have to travel greater distances to find food. Since koalas are better climbers than walkers, traveling long distances is dangerous. Koalas risk being attacked by dogs or hit by cars. Australian citizens are helping by keeping their pets in at night and planting feeding trees. They are even posting "Koala crossing" signs for drivers and working to pass laws protecting forests.

Because conditions are often very dry, brush fires in Australia can be ferocious, fast-moving, and very dangerous to humans and animals.

ACCIDENTS AND ABANDONMENT

Gone with the wind

Sometimes animals are faced with freak accidents. In 2009 Tinkerbell, a tiny, 2.7-kilogram (6-pound) Chihuahua, was strolling around a Michigan flea market with her owners. Suddenly, a huge gust of wind blew. It knocked tiny Tinkerbell off her feet and swept her away—far away! After two days of searching, her owners consulted a pet expert, who directed them to a wooded area about 1.6 kilometers (1 mile) away. There was Tinkerbell. She was hungry and dirty, but very happy to see her owners.

A flush with death

In 2009, in London, four-year-old Daniel Blair thought his puppy needed a bath. So, Daniel gave Dyno, a week-old cocker spaniel, a wash . . . in the toilet. And then he flushed. Daniel's mother, Alison, said, "I ran to the bathroom, but the dog was nowhere to be seen. I assumed it was dead. I went into the garden, managed to lift up the drain cover, and was amazed to hear him crying."

Tinkerbell the dog, safe in her owner's arms after a windy adventure.

SURVIVAL FACT

It is rare for animals—even tiny ones like Tinkerbell—to be carried away by the wind. Usually it takes gusts from a tropical storm or tornado to move a living creature. But the 112-kilometers-per-hour (70-miles-per-hour) winds that Tinkerbell experienced were as strong as some **hurricanes** or tornadoes.

But reaching Dyno was not easy. The dog had been swept almost 18 meters (20 yards) from the Blairs' toilet to a pipe underneath a neighbor's house. A plumber placed a special camera in the pipe to see where the dog was. He used his equipment to push the dog toward a manhole cover. When Dyno was close enough, a firefighter grabbed the puppy. He was wet and muddy, but okay.

Dyno, the cocker spaniel puppy, after surviving a wet and wild trip down the toilet.

Abandoned: Knut the polar bear

Thomas Doerflein was the chief bear keeper at the Berlin Zoo, in Germany. On December 5, 2006, a polar bear named Tosca gave birth to two cubs. But Thomas worried that Tosca, raised in a zoo, might not know how to take care of her babies. He waited, but Tosca showed little interest in the cubs.

Thomas would need to raise the pair himself. It would be a tough job. One of every two polar bears born in **captivity** dies—even with a mother's around-the-clock care. Without a mother, zookeepers must spend every moment with the cubs, acting just like a real polar bear parent.

Berlin Zoo bear keeper Thomas Doerflein with Knut, the polar bear cub he raised.

Thomas put the cubs, which were the size of guinea pigs, in a heated bed called an incubator to raise their body temperatures. Then he created a special formula for the cubs, which he fed to them every two hours. Mothers do not leave their cubs' sides until they are three months old. So, Thomas moved a bed and sleeping bag into the cubs' room, where he could tend to them night and day. Thomas brushed them with baby oil, bathed them, and changed their bedding. On the fourth day, one of the cubs died. But the other one grew stronger. When it was a month old, Thomas named it Knut.

Knut becomes famous

Soon, Knut took his first wobbly steps and began to wrestle, pounce, and roll in the sand. In March 2007, Knut and Thomas drew hundreds of fans and photographers when they appeared for the first time in public. A few months later, Thomas received Berlin's Medal of Merit award for his dedication in raising Knut from a tiny cub to a healthy, 80-kilogram (176-pound) bear.

Sadly, Thomas died the following year of a sudden heart attack. But he had completed his job. At 22 months, Knut was able to survive without his beloved foster parent. Knut continues to warm the hearts of his adoring fans at the Berlin Zoo. Even so, it can be hard for even the best zoo to give an adult male polar bear everything he needs. Knut's natural territory would cover hundreds of square miles!

SURVIVAL SCIENCE

Polar bear survival

The number of polar bears in existence has decreased in the past 20 years. This is because rising temperatures in the Arctic have melted much of the ice that polar bears use as their base for hunting and fishing. Polar bears are now considered a "threatened" **species**. If the warming trend continues at its current pace, polar bears could become **extinct** (die out) by the end of the century. Zoos can help protect polar bears. And everyday people can help reverse the warming trend by doing things to help the environment, such as planting trees, using cars less and bicycles more, and recycling.

INCREDIBLE JOURNEYS

How far will an animal go to be reunited with its owner? The animals in these stories went to great lengths to return to the people and places they call home.

Bobbie's incredible journey

In 1923 the Brazier family brought their dog, Bobbie (a collie-shepherd mix) with them on a trip from their home in Oregon to the East Coast of the United States. While they were in Indiana, some local dogs started chasing the collie. By the time Bobbie outran the dogs, he was lost. His owners searched for days, but finally moved on. Bobbie moved on, too. His journey was pieced together later by people who remembered meeting him. Many of them offered Bobbie food and invited him in. But Bobbie kept heading west. He crossed rivers and plains. He hunted rabbits and herded sheep. He fought wolves and ran with them. Once, he got caught in a farmer's wolf trap. Then the farmer hung him on a rope as wolf bait. He was saved by a wolf he had befriended earlier.

Six months after he was lost, Bobbie—with swollen legs, a matted coat, and bloody paws—limped into the Braziers' house in Oregon. He had traveled almost 4,800 kilometers (3,000 miles)! He soon became known as "Bobbie the Wonder Dog."

SURVIVAL SCIENCE

How do animals find their way?

How did Bobbie find his way home? The answer is still a mystery. Many dogs have made similar journeys, but this is one of the most extreme. It is possible that some dogs have inherited the ability to create "mental maps" from their **ancestors**. Long ago, dogs' lives depended on being able to return to their territories after traveling long distances to hunt. Scientists believe that dogs can still create "maps" of their environment by carefully observing the land around them with their super-strong senses of sight, smell, and hearing. It is also possible that, like birds, dogs are able to sense Earth's **magnetic fields** (see page 13). This would always let them know which direction they are headed.

A picture of Bobbie, the dog who walked across the United States in search of his beloved owners.

Nubs the war dog

The journey of Nubs the dog began in 2007, on the cold desert sands of western Iraq. That is where the stray dog wandered into a U.S. Marine fort—and into Major Brian Dennis's life. The dog looked hungry, so Brian shared his food with the dog and scratched his belly. Brian named the dog Nubs, because he had just two little nubs for ears (see the box below). Nubs followed Brian on his night patrols. Together, they kept the fort safe. But Brian often had to return to his command post, where no dogs were allowed.

One night, Brian found Nubs limping and whimpering. The dog had been stabbed in the side with a screwdriver. Nubs was in such agony he would not eat, drink, or even lie down. Brian cleaned the wound and force-fed the dog medicine to heal the infection. Brian slept next to Nubs to warm the dog and woke frequently to check on him. "I really expected when I woke up for watch he would be dead," said Brian. "Somehow he made it through the night."

Nubs warmly welcomes Brian upon his arrival in San Diego.

NUBS'S NUBS

Before Nubs came into Brian's life, he was a wild, alert-dog for Iraqi soldiers. He lived a rough life with other street dogs, making noise when strangers approached. His ears were probably cut off to make him look tougher and to give other dogs less to grab ahold of in a fight!

Nubs's journey

Brian had to leave Nubs and return to his command post the next day. But Nubs was not about to lose Brian again. The dog hobbled across freezing desert sands and past packs of wild dogs, in search of his friend. Two days and 112 kilometers (70 miles) later, Nubs limped his way into the outpost—and into Brian's arms! Brian and most of his colleagues welcomed the dog. But a few soldiers complained, so Brian's bosses said he had four days to get rid of

Nubs—or the dog would be shot. Brian emailed his colleagues, friends, and family. Together they gathered enough money to give Nubs a new life in Brian's hometown of San Diego, California.

Nubs was flown all the way from the neighboring country of Jordan to Chicago, and then to San Diego, California—a journey of thousands of miles (see the map). A month later, Brian joined the dog. "Nubs went crazy," says Brian. "He was jumping up on me, licking my head." Brian took Nubs to one of his favorite beaches in San Diego. There, Nubs wandered with Brian in the warm sand, thousands of miles from where his journey began.

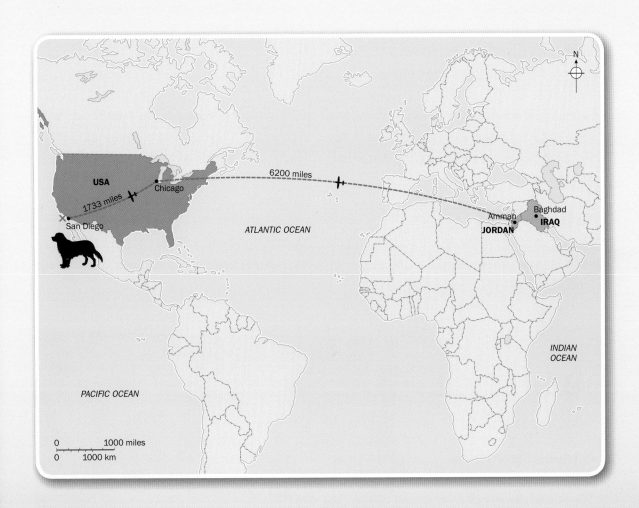

Bird brain

In 2008 the police were at a loss. They found an African Gray parrot on a rooftop in Tokyo, Japan. They took it to the station, but they had no way to identify the bird. The following day, they transferred the parrot to an animal hospital. There, the speckled gray bird started greeting people by name and singing popular children's songs. After a few days, it started talking. One day, the bird announced, "I'm Mr. Yosuke Nakamura" and recited a full address. Workers checked the street number. Sure enough, a "Nakamura" family lived there. The Nakamuras, it seems, had spent over two years teaching the bird to recite his name and address, in case he ever got lost. The police returned the bird to the happy owners.

The blue parakeet

A young girl in Arizona thought it would be fun to play outside with her sister's bright-blue parakeet. The bird's wings were clipped. But as soon as the parakeet reached the yard, he shot up into the sky and disappeared in a whirl of blue feathers. The young girl began to cry. She worried that her sister would never forgive her, but instead her sister tried to comfort her. "Maybe he will survive," she said. But both sisters knew that a parakeet that had always lived in a cage could not survive long on its own. It would not know how to feed itself or keep itself warm at night.

Years later, when the young girl was an adult, she and a new friend told each other childhood pet stories. The friend said his favorite pet had been a blue parakeet that had come into his life in a peculiar way. He was in his yard one day, when the bird just floated down from the clear-blue sky and perched itself on his finger. After comparing dates, the young woman concluded that the man's bird was her sister's lost blue pet! Not only had the bird survived, he had lived a long life.

SURVIVAL SCIENCE

An intelligent bird

The African Gray parrot is one of the world's most intelligent birds. Scientists think that it has the language abilities of a young child.

Yosuke Nakamura survived getting lost in the big city of Toyko by reciting his own address!

SURVIVAL SCIENCE

Trust

The parakeet had been trained to trust and depend on humans. This is probably why he flew right to the finger of another human.

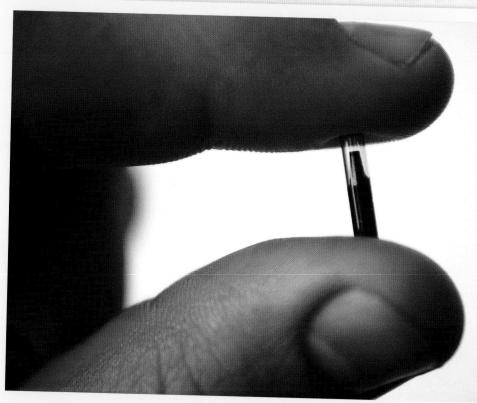

Pet microchips like this one help reunite hundreds of lost or stolen pets with their owners every year.

MICROCHIPS

Today, identifying a lost pet can be very easy. Pet owners just need to plant a **microchip**—about the size of a large grain of rice—under their pet's skin. When the pet is "scanned," the microchip number is retrieved, and the owner's contact information can be found.

WITH A LITTLE HELP FROM THEIR FRIENDS

Will animals do anything in order to survive, even if it means killing their brother or cousin? It seems the opposite is often true. Many animals are social creatures. They live in groups, where they play with each other, hunt together, and help one another defend their territory. These bonds can make animals loyal friends. As these stories show, they can also make animals great survivors.

Tika and Kobuk: In sickness and in health

The dogs Kobuk and Tika had been companions for years. Together, the two malamutes had bred and raised eight litters of puppies. But Kobuk, the male dog, still sometimes acted like an overgrown puppy himself. He would eat Tika's food before she could get to it and knock Tika over if she was in his way. If people tried to pet or play with Tika, Kobuk shoved himself in between. Kobuk wanted all eyes (and hands) on himself. Until Tika got sick, that is.

When Tika was diagnosed with a cancerous tumor on her leg, Kobuk's behavior changed overnight. He began grooming Tika's ears and face. He let Tika sleep on the bed, while he camped out on the floor below. He stayed by her side. When Tika's leg was **amputated**, Kobuk tried to help her up when she fell.

One night, Kobuk started barking. Then, Anne Bekoff, the dogs' owner, heard Tika whining softly. She looked at Tika's belly and saw that it was swollen. Tika was going into shock! Anne got Tika to an emergency veterinary clinic just in time. Anne said, "If Kobuk hadn't fetched me from sleep, Tika almost certainly would have died before I realized anything was wrong."

After Tika healed from surgery and learned to walk on three legs, Kobuk went back to his old, rude ways. But not until he had saved Tika's life.

Malamutes Tika and Kobuk helped prove that it's not always a "dog-eat-dog" world, by helping each other when it counted most.

Echo and Ely the elephants

Ely the elephant was born in 1990 in Kenya. Most elephants learn to walk just 30 minutes after being born, but Ely struggled. The lower part of Ely's front legs were bent back like backward "Ls" and would not straighten. Ely's mother, Echo, and his older sister, Enid, stayed with Ely while the other elephants set off to find food, water, and shade from the hot sun. They protected him from other herds of elephants and encouraged him to walk. By day three, Ely's legs started to straighten and he finally stood, thanks in part to his family's love and patience.

SURVIVAL SCIENCE

Maternal bonds

Baby elephants stay inside their mothers for 22 months. They nurse as long as 4 years. During that time, the mothers and babies develop an extremely strong bond. This explains why Echo put herself in danger to protect Ely.

When Ely was seven years old, he was struck in the back by a spear. He bled for several days before a veterinary team arrived to remove the spear. To calm Ely for the operation, the vet put him temporarily to sleep with a tranquilizer dart. When Ely dropped to the ground, his elephant family surrounded him. The team tried to chase the elephants away, but Echo and Enid stood firm, even in the face of an SUV driving quickly toward them. Eventually the team was able to help Ely, but the other elephants refused to move until Ely's surgery was successfully completed.

Tarra and Bella

When Tarra the elephant was retired from the circus, she was placed in a safe home called the Elephant Sanctuary, in Hohenwald, Tennessee. But she did not fit in there. All the other elephants found a best friend, but not Tarra. That is, until she met a stray dog named Bella.

Soon the two were never apart. But in 2008, the park rangers found Tarra alone. Bella was lying in the grass a few feet away with a spinal cord injury. She became **paralyzed** and could not move her legs or wag her tail. During the three weeks that Bella was in the sanctuary's medical center, Tarra stayed where she was. She had thousands of acres to roam, but she would not move. One day, the doctors put Bella on a balcony, so that she could see Tarra. For the first time, Bella's tail began to wag again. After that, the two visited each other every day until Bella was back on her feet. The two remain best friends.

Tarra the elephant towers over her friend, Bella the dog.

ANIMAL HEROES

Animals can survive in difficult situations. They can also be heroes. The dogs, cats, and dolphins in these stories are just a few of the many brave animals that have saved the lives of others.

Norman: Dark victory

When Annette McDonald adopted Norman from a local Oregon animal shelter, he seemed like a perfectly healthy puppy. But after a few months, the blonde Labrador started bumping into doors and furniture. A veterinarian discovered that Norman had a rare disease, which would cause his vision to decline. Soon he would be blind for life.

Norman seemed most comfortable near the water, or at the beach, with its long, clear coastline. One day in 1996, Annette watched as Norman raced straight into a cold river. He began swimming out into the river—something Annette did not even know the dog could do. Then Annette saw something else. A young girl was way out in the river, bobbing up and down. Norman must have heard her calling. The drowning girl grabbed Norman's tail, and Norman began pulling her to shore. But the girl's grip slipped. The dog sniffed to find her, but her scent was lost. From the shore, Annette yelled, "He's blind. Call his name! It's Norman." The girl shouted "Norman!" The dog followed the girl's voice and dragged her safely to shore.

Norman's sharp hearing abilities helped him hear a young girl calling out for help.

SURVIVAL SCIENCE

Losing a sense

Dogs can hear sounds at distances four times greater than humans. But that was not the whole story with Norman. When animals—or people—lose one sense, some evidence suggests that other senses can become sharper. For instance, a blind animal sometimes hears better than one that can see. Norman's blindness might have helped him find the girl. Without anything to look at, Norman probably listened more carefully to the sounds around him.

Hero cat: Cool in a crisis

The calico cat had no home. So, in 1996 she gave birth to her five kittens in an abandoned building in Brooklyn, New York. After a few days, the mother cat left her kittens in a cozy bundle while she went to find food. When she returned, smoke was pouring out of the building. It was on fire! Firefighters aimed their hoses at the flames, but the kittens were still trapped inside. The mother cat dashed into the building, picked up one of them in her teeth, and dropped it on the wet grass outside. Then she went back for another. And another. Soon flames blocked the doorway and shot up from the floor. The mother pushed through the fire, severely burning herself, but rescued the final two kittens, which were barely breathing.

SURVIVAL SCIENCE

Hormones

When nursing, cats' bodies release a **hormone** that strengthens the bond they have with their babies. This helps explain why the mother cat put herself in harm's way to protect her kittens.

A veterinary worker tends to Scarlett, who was injured saving her kittens from a fire.

A firefighter found the cats and took them to an animal shelter to recover. He named the courageous mother cat Scarlett, for the flames that she braved to save her little ones. Newspapers and television stations reported the story, and people lined up to adopt the cat and her kittens. The mother cat's rescue not only saved her kittens' lives. It also helped find them homes.

Flippered friends

In 2007 Todd Endris experienced a shock. One minute, the surfer was riding the waves off the coast of Monterey, California, with dolphins frolicking nearby. The next minute, an enormous great white shark loomed over the surfer's head, like an image from a horror movie. The giant fish opened its jaws wide and bit down on Todd and his surfboard, trapping him in its giant clutches. Its teeth scraped skin off Todd's back. Then, the shark's teeth gripped Todd's leg, while Todd used his other leg to kick the shark in the face.

Dolphins have been known to protect surfers from danger.

That is when the dolphins moved in. Before the shark could continue attacking, the dolphins stopped playing and formed a ring around Todd. Their formation protected Todd from the shark and allowed him to paddle safely to shore. Todd lost half of his blood and required over 500 stitches and 200 staples to close his wounds. But he survived and was even able to surf again a few months later.

SURVIVAL SCIENCE

The human connection

Scientists are not sure why dolphins protect humans. But stories of dolphins helping humans date back to ancient times. In 2006 four lifeguards in New Zealand were also saved from sharks by dolphins forming a protective ring.

Trixie and the toilet bowl

In 1992, when Jack Fyfe woke up, he could not move. The 75-year-old resident of Sydney, Australia, had suffered a **stroke** during the night. This sudden loss of brain function left him completely **paralyzed**. Jack lived alone, and the stroke left him unable to use the telephone. So, Jack called out to his sheepdog, Trixie, and asked the pet to bring him water. And, amazingly, the dog obeyed!

Trixie found a towel, soaked it in her water dish, and brought it back to Jack. Trixie even draped the towel over Jack's mouth so he could suck out the moisture. Days went by, and Trixie kept up the ritual. After her water dish was empty, Trixie began soaking the towel in the toilet bowl. It was nine days before a relative noticed that Jack was missing and came to check on him. Jack was weak, but thanks to a very clever sheepdog, still alive. Without Trixie and the water she brought, Jack would have died.

George, the cancer-sniffing dog

George the dog had a successful career helping people. Using his good sense of smell, he helped Florida police officers find bombs. But in the early 1990s, George also learned how to

Trixie, a kelpie-border collie mix, understood the word "water."

detect cancer. A trainer waved a test tube filled with cancerous cells under the schnauzer's nose. George would know exactly what to sniff for. Then, George was put to the test. He was brought to an examining table, where a man named Eddie lay, dressed in a bathing suit and covered with bandages. The trainer had placed cancerous cells under just one of the bandages. It was George's job to figure out which one.

But instead of picking out the bandage with the cancerous cells, George went straight to a patch covering up a freckle. Eddie's doctor had told him the spot was harmless. But George kept sniffing and pawing at the bandage with such purpose that Eddie had the freckle re-examined. It was discovered that he had a life-threatening form of skin cancer. If the "freckle" had not been treated, Eddie could have died within a year.

SURVIVAL SCIENCE

Can animals detect disease?

A dog's sense of smell is 10,000 times greater than a human's. Many dogs, like George, have alerted owners to tumors by pawing at cancerous growths. Scientists also believe that dogs can actually smell a person's blood. This is good news for diabetics, people who have a difficult time regulating their blood sugar levels. Trained dogs can alert their owners before their blood sugar reaches a dangerous point.

Cancer-sniffing dogs are trained to sniff out cancer cells in containers like these.

Like these workers, Mike and Roselle ran from the World Trade Center towers in New York, shortly before they collapsed.

Roselle: Fearless leader

Mike Hingson could hear the explosion and the screams. He could feel the entire building shake, sway, and then straighten itself. But since he was blind, Mike could not see what came afterward. Dark-gray smoke billowed out from the damaged building, while red flames gobbled up glass and melted metal. He could not see the loose papers and debris that rained down from the sky. The date was September 11, 2001. Mike was working on the 78th floor of the World Trade Center when terrorists crashed airplanes into the towers.

If Mike was going to get out alive, he would need to use a different set of eyes: those of Roselle, his service dog. He could feel Roselle's tail striking steadily against his leg. The dog seemed calm, which soothed Mike's nerves. But the trip down the long stairwell was difficult. Roselle paused for rescue workers and when people started shoving and shouting. But Mike kept directing her down all 77 floors, until finally they reached the exit.

Outside, Mike heard the other tower rumble. Someone shouted, "Run! It's coming down!" Mike ordered Roselle to "hop up," or go faster. They ran as the tower crumbled behind them. Even returning to Mike's home in New Jersey was tough. The subway was shut down, so Mike and Roselle had to walk for hours until they found a working train. Roselle later received a medal for her heroic actions that day.

SURVIVAL SCIENCE

Follow the leader

In the wild, dogs run in packs led by one dog. Since dogs are used to following a leader, they can learn to follow human orders, too. Roselle was a trained service dog. At just eight weeks, she learned basic skills, like sitting, staying, and being friendly. At 18 months, she learned more advanced skills, including walking in a straight line, stopping at curbs, and going up and down stairs at a steady pace. All of this training paid off as Roselle helped Mike survive the tragedy of September 11.

Mike with Roselle, the service dog that led him to safety during a terrorist attack.

Learning from animals

We may never know exactly why animals do everything they do. But we can learn a lot from watching what animals do. In these true stories, we have seen animals adjusting to difficult, new conditions. We have witnessed animals using their super-senses to detect danger. We have watched animals putting their lives at risk to take care of their young. We have observed animals forming bonds with other animals or humans to protect each other from danger. All of these actions contributed to the animals' own survival or the survival of others. As humans, we can relate to these behaviors. And we can also learn from them. After all, humans are animals, too.

MORE ANIMAL SURVIVAL FACTS

Birds of war: Extreme survival

In World War I (1914–18) and World War II (1939–45), militaries trained homing pigeons. They used these birds to transport important messages when radio communication was impossible or dangerous. A small capsule with a paper message inside was attached to the leg of the pigeon. The bird was then released to fly to the raised shelter where it lived.

But the pigeons' missions were filled with danger. Many pigeons did not successfully return home. Many were shot down by enemy shooters or attacked by falcons trained by the enemy. Others died as a result of bad weather, wild birds, or exhaustion.

Mary of Exeter

Throughout World War II, a pigeon named Mary of Exeter was repeatedly dropped in France. There, she would receive a top-secret message, then return it to her home in England. It seemed that nothing could stop the little gray bird. Once, Mary was shot and had to undergo an operation to remove pellets from her body. Another time, Mary was assumed dead after not returning. But four days later, she staggered home, matted with blood. A hawk had torn her open from her neck to her breast, nearly ripping off her wing.

TOP SECRET

She was stitched up, only to be hit by bullet fragments during a bomb raid. The fragments damaged her head and neck. But her owner, a shoemaker, created a leather collar for the pigeon. Mary was one of 32 pigeons awarded a medal for bravery.

AMAZING VISION

Pigeons can see as far as 16 kilometers (10 miles) in the distance, even in fog. Because of this, they are often used to find men and women lost at sea. In World War II, specially trained pigeons rode in the bellies of rescue planes. They would peck a button if they spotted the orange survival vest of a fallen pilot.

AMAZING ANIMAL SENSES: A COMPARISON

	HUMANS	CATS	DOGS	THE WINNER IS
HEARING	64-23,000 Hz	45-64,000 Hz **WINNER**	40-60,000 Hz	Cats have the best hearing, followed by dogs, then humans.
SMELL	5 million odor-sensing cells	200 million odor-sensing cells	220 million odor-sensing cells **WINNER**	Dogs have the best sense of smell by a whisker over cats. Humans lag far behind.
TASTE	10,000 taste buds **WINNER**	473 taste buds	1,700 taste buds	Humans win here, meaning we notice differences between how things taste. Dogs and cats tell more about their food from smelling, rather than tasting it.
SIGHT	20/20	20/100	20/75	Depending on how you "see" things, humans have better vision than cats and dogs. But both cats and dogs see better in the dark. In fact, cats see six times better than humans in the dark.

WINNER?

GLOSSARY

adapt get used to something or change in a way that allows you to survive in a new situation

amputate cut off an arm, leg, or other limb in surgery

ancestor relative from the past

bush forested wilderness in Australia

captivity state of being confined, such as when an animal is raised by humans

electromagnetic wave wave of electric and magnetic energy

endangered in danger of dying out

epicenter area of Earth's surface directly above the place where an earthquake starts

evacuate leave an area for safety reasons

extinct when a species has completely died out

habitat animal's natural surroundings

hormone substance formed by certain cells that has a specific effect on the body

hurricane violent, tropical storm, having wind speeds of 119 kilometers per hour (74 miles per hour) or greater

instinct ability to respond to a situation without thinking about what to do

magnetic field invisible area surrounding Earth that has the effect of the pull of a magnet

magnetite hard, black mineral that is strongly attracted by magnets

microchip circuit placed under the skin of an animal to help identify it

migrate move from one region to another with the change in seasons

paralyzed unable to move some part of the body. Paralysis can be temporary or permanent.

pride group of lions

prosthesis device that substitutes for a missing part of the body

species specific group of animals that are related

stroke sudden loss of brain function that occurs when blood flow to the brain is restricted. It can result in memory loss, speech impairment, temporary or permanent paralysis, or death.

tsunami huge sea wave produced by an underwater earthquake or undersea volcanic eruption

FIND OUT MORE

BOOKS

Bourke, Anthony, and John Rendall. *Christian the Lion*. New York, NY: Henry Holt, 2009.

Burnford, Sheila Every. *The Incredible Journey*. New York, NY: Delacorte Books for Young Readers, 1996.

Dennis, Brian, Kirby Larson, and Mary Nethery. *Nubs: A Mutt*, a Marine & a Miracle. New York, NY: Little, Brown, 2009.

Halls, Kelly Milner, and William Sumner. *Saving the Baghdad Zoo: A True Story of Hope and Heroes*. New York, NY: Greenwillow, 2010.

Hatkoff, Juliana et al. *Knut: How One Little Polar Bear Captivated the World*. New York, NY: Scholastic, 2007.

Kaster, Pam. *Molly the Pony: A True Story*. Baton Rouge, LA: Louisiana State University Press, 2008.

Larson, Kirby and Mary Nethery. *Two Bobbies: A True Story of Hurricane Katrina, Friendship, and Survival*. New York, NY: Macmillan, 2008.

Markle, Sandra. *Animal Heroes: True Rescue Stories*. Minneapolis, MN: Millbrook, 2009.

DVDS

Christian the Lion: The Lion Who Thought He Was People. La Jolla, CA: Hollywood Select, 1971. This movie is based on the true story of Christian the lion.

Eight Below. Burbank, CA: Disney, 2006. This Disney film is inspired by the Japanese expedition to Antarctica and the sled dogs that were left behind.

Fly Away Home. Culver City, CA: Columbia Pictures, 1996. This tale of a young girl and her Canada geese is based on the story of Bill Lishman and his migration experiments.

Homeward Bound: The Incredible Journey. Burbank, CA: Disney, 1993. This movie is based on the true story of Bobbie the collie.

WEBSITES

www.twobobbies.com

This is the website for the book *Two Bobbies*. Find extra information about Bob the cat, Bobbi the dog, Hurricane Katrina, and more.

www.aspca.org

This is the website for the American Society for the Prevention of Cruelty to Animals (ASPCA). Find out more information about stopping animal cruelty, adopting animals, and caring for pets.

http://polarbearsinternational.org

This is the website of the conservation group Polar Bears International. Learn all about polar bears, how to "adopt" a polar bear, and how to make the world safer for polar bears.

INDEX

abandonment 18, 22, 30–31
accidents 28–29
Ace (actor) 10, 11
Adamson family 10
adaptation 11, 22
African Gray parrots 36
Antarctica 6
Australia 8–9, 26, 27, 46

Baghdad Zoo 22
Barnett, Bill 23
Beauty (dog) 23
Bekoff, Anne 38
Bella (dog) 41
Berlin Zoo 30–31
Blair family 28
"the Blitz" 23
Bobbie (dog) 32
Bobbi Dog 19
Bob Cat 19
brush fires 26, 27

cancer 38, 46–47
cats 19, 23, 44, 51
China 14–15
Christian (lion) 10–11
Cinders (koala) 26
Congo 24

Dennis, Brian 34–35
diabetes 47
diseases 42
Dixon Correctional Facility 21
Doerflein, Thomas 30–31
dogs 6, 7, 8–9, 19, 21, 23, 27,
    28–29, 32, 34–35, 38, 41, 42,
    43, 46–47, 48–49, 51
dolphins 44–45
Dyno (dog) 28–29

earthquakes 14, 15, 16
Echo (elephant) 40
electromagnetic waves 14
elephants 40, 41
Elephant Sanctuary 41
Ely (elephant) 40
Endris, Todd 44–45
eucalyptus trees 26, 27

fires 26, 27, 44
Frisky (dog) 21
Fyfe, Jack 46

geese 12–13
George (disaster survivor) 21
George (dog) 46–47
Germany 23, 30–31
Griffith family 8–9

Hingson, Mike 48–49
hippos 16–17
homing pigeons 50
hormones 44
hunting 6, 7, 8, 9, 10, 19, 24, 26,
    27, 31, 32, 38
Hurricane Katrina 18, 19, 20, 21
huskies 6, 7

illness 38, 46–47
instinct 5, 8
Iraq 22, 34

Jiro (sled dog) 6, 7
John (actor) 10, 11
journeys 32, 34–35, 36, 37

Kabirizi (gorilla) 24
Kenya 10, 11, 16–17, 40
Knut (polar bear) 30–31
koalas 26, 27
Kobuk (dog) 38

Lessinjina (gorilla) 24
Lishman, Bill 12–13

magnetic fields 13, 32
magnetite 13
maps 8, 35
Mary of Exeter (pigeon) 50
McDonald, Annette 42
microchips 37
migration 12–13
Miza (gorilla) 24
Molly (pony) 20
mountain gorillas 24
Mzee (tortoise) 17

Nakamura family 36

natural disasters 14–15, 16, 17, 18,
    19, 20, 21, 26, 27, 28
Norman (dog) 42, 43
Nubs (dog) 34–35

Owen (hippo) 16–17

Palmer, Richard 21
pandas 14–15
Papi (dog) 21
parakeets 36, 37
parrots 36
pelicans 22
People's Dispensary for Sick Animals
    23
polar bears 30, 31
prosthetic limbs 20

Roselle (dog) 48–49

Scarlett (cat) 44
search and rescue 23, 50
senses 5, 13, 14, 32, 42, 43,
    46–47, 51
September 11 attacks 48–49
service dogs 48–49
shark attacks 44–45
sled dogs 6, 7
Sophie (dog) 8–9
Sumner, William 22

Taro (sled dog) 6, 7
Tarra (elephant) 41
Tika (dog) 38
Tinkerbell (dog) 28
tortoises 17
Tosca (polar bear) 30
travel. See journeys.
Trixie (dog) 46
trust 36, 37
tsunamis 16, 17

Virunga Park 24

warming trend 31
whooping cranes 13
Wolong National Nature Reserve
    14–15
World War I/II 50